The Survival Rate
of Butterflies in the Wild

The Survival Rate
of Butterflies in the Wild

Murray Reiss

HAGIOS PRESS
Box 33024 Cathedral PO
Regina SK S4T 7X2
www.hagiospress.com

Copyright © 2013 Murray Reiss

All rights reserved. No part of this publication may be reproduced, stored in a retrieval system, or transmitted in any form or by any means without the prior written permission of the publisher or by licensed agreement with Access: The Canadian Copyright Licensing Agency. Exceptions will be made in the case of a reviewer, who may quote brief passages in a review to print in a magazine or newspaper, broadcast on radio or television, or post on the Internet.

Library and Archives Canada Cataloguing in Publication

Reiss, Murray
 The survival rate of butterflies in the wild / Murray Reiss.

(Strike fire new authors series)

Poems.
ISBN 978-1-926710-20-4

I. Title. II. Series: Strike fire new authors series
 PS8635.E485S97 2012   C811'.6   C2012-905470-4

Edited by Paul Wilson.
Designed and typeset by Donald Ward.
Cover art: "The Family," by Samuel Bak, courtesy of Pucker Gallery, Boston, MA.
Cover Design: Tania Wolk, Go Giraffe Go Inc.
Set in Adobe Caslon Pro.
Printed and bound in Canada.

The publishers gratefully acknowledge the assistance of the Saskatchewan Arts Board, The Canada Council for the Arts, and the Creative Industry Growth and Sustainability program, made possible through funding provided to the Saskatchewan Arts Board by the Government of Saskatchewan through the Ministry of Tourism, Parks, Culture and Sport.

For Karen and Kaya

These poems have appeared in the following magazines, anthologies, and chapbooks, sometimes in a slightly different form:

Vintage 97–98: "Unanswered Letters"
CV2: "My Grandmother's Hair"
Great Lakes logia & *Literal Latte*: "The Perfect Stone"
Distance From the Locus: "The Perfect Stone," "Mannequins' Graveyard," "Unanswered Letters," "Station Scarecrow Twin"

The Survival Rate of Butterflies in the Wild was completed with the aid of a grant from the Canada Council.

Contents

Multiple Choice   9

STARVED FOR WORDS

Starved for Words   13
Shut up, Please, I'm Not Talking   14
Wet Matches   16
Ferry   19
Runaways   20
Aneurysm   22
Traces   23

RIDDLE AND DITCH

My Father's Eyes in Poland: Riddle and Ditch   27

ALTERATIONS

My Grandmother's Sewing Machine   35
Anne in the Attic   37
My Grandmother's Hair   38
Kaput   39
Mannequins' Graveyard   42
The Perfect Stone   44
Unanswered Letters   46
Buried in a Book   47
Whittled and Fed   49
Big Tomatoes   50

THE SURVIVAL RATE OF BUTTERFLIES IN THE WILD

The Survival Rate of Butterflies in the Wild   53

SECOND-HAND SURVIVOR

Second-hand Survivor   65
Empty Frames   66
Prayer   67
Who Could Argue?   68
Faces like Mine   70
Earliest Rivals   71
Blunt Shovel   73
The Last Two Jews in Poland   74

STATION, SCARECROW, TWIN

In Poland before I Was Born: Clubfoot Twin   79
Mengele Had to Love   81
Under the Wire   83
Boarding Time   85
How to Play Hunt and Hide   86
Station, Scarecrow, Twin   88
Postcards from Poland: Prayers   90
Father Your Village   91

Notes   93
Glossary   94

MULTIPLE CHOICE

After everyone my father:
   a) loved
   b) left behind
was:
   a) gassed
      at: i) Belzec
          ii) Chelmno
          iii) Sobibor
          iv) Treblinka
          v) Auschwitz
or:
   b) shot
      i) in their beds
      ii) in the street
      iii) at worship
      iv) in a hiding place betrayed by:
         1) a Polish peasant
         2) another Jew
         3) blind bad luck
or:
   c) died of typhus
      in: one of (a) above
or:
   d) died of starvation
      in: i) the Lodz ghetto
         ii) the Vilna ghetto
         iii) the Lublin ghetto
         iv) the Warsaw ghetto
or:
   e) died in the boxcar
      on the way to one of (a) above

   or: _____/ none of the above —

he never said a word about them.

He carried them all to his grave
as if believing that
closing his fists on their lives without letting a drop:
    (a) spill out or
    (b) ooze between his fingers
was
    (c) the only way to keep
     them his.

STARVED FOR WORDS

STARVED FOR WORDS

My mother had no
milk nor my father
words. That's how it was
in the century's middle
when history's branding
iron cauterized
his tongue.

No one expected luxuries,
like a world
that made sense.
You settled for crumbs
and thanked
your lucky stars.

Nothing was ever
over — least of all
the smoke.
Every closet hid
its shovel, every drawer
a hatchet or two.

He stuffed his past
in a burlap bag and drowned
it like kittens. It sank
to the bottom of the well.

What's the matter, his eyes
would taunt me — Cat
got your tongue?

SHUT UP, PLEASE, I'M NOT TALKING

After the disaster
only money talked.

The dead stubbed out
their tongues
and kept on walking.

Who knew how to bury
puffs of smoke?

☙

In his silence my father
became a word-
less poet. Every end-
stopped breath
a rhyme for death.

☙

It always walked
behind us.
Its penumbra
always fell two
steps ahead.

☙

It wasn't grunts.
It wasn't gnashing or savage music.

It wasn't a wordless wailing
for the dead.

It wasn't the language even the dead
can't stop rehearsing, their long repetitive
solos, drums
and the clarinet's wail.

It wasn't the stut-
ter of peb-
bles rat-
tling in his throat.

It was the only way
he could say what
couldn't be said.

Some families bury stones
when they have no bodies.

He buried every word
they ever spoke.

WET MATCHES

not knowing how to live
I went searching for ancestral wisdom

not knowing where to look
I turned to my father's dead

giving them their first good laugh in years

> *we're dead you fool*
> *in case you haven't noticed*

dead or alive
it makes no difference to me
I want your teachings

> *teachings what teachings*
> *we were peddlers not rabbis*
> *you want blond wigs*
> *to hide those coal-black curls*
> *we got*

it's all right
my hair's already fair

> *you want a little foreskin*
> *stick it on your* petseleh
> *fool the* goyim *when they pull down your pants*
> *(so long as they don't yank too hard)*
> *we got that too*

they don't do that here
no one's going to pull down my pants
to inspect my dick

> *prayer books*
> *fake passports*
> *matches by the cartload*
> *(okay they're a little damp*
> *so buy in bulk and you get a discount)*
> *boychik let me tell you*
> *this is your lucky day*
> *from now until midnight*
> *is our closing out sale*
> *everything we got it's got to go*
> *you got a horse you can haul it away right now*
> *you don't got a horse we'll find you a good one cheap*

my ancestral dead
disconcertingly like my father
they're as willing in death as in life
to strike a deal …

> *why don't you go ask your father*
> *last we looked*
> *he was still alive*

> *first he gets lucky then he gets rich*
> *you want to know how to live*
> *and you don't ask him*

he knows how to make a living
I want to know how to live

> *boychik, you think there's a difference?*
> *if we knew better how to make a living*
> *maybe we'd still be alive*

but if I don't know where I came from
how can I know who I am

you want to know your roots
ask him where we're buried

never mind we don't have bodies
look around

we'll throw in
a deal on shovels
two for one

side by side
with shovels like these
(for you we'll rub off the rust
even straighten the handles)
who knows what you might
dig up

FERRY

Yiddish was my parents' secret
language. They used it to tell
each other what couldn't be told.

Zsackschovickoykhurbnoyvaysmir…
Its syllables had an aura
that made me cringe.

There is always another world
even worse than this one. The boat
that ferries us back and forth
is full of holes.

RUNAWAYS

My father saved
my life when he crossed
the ocean.

By the time
I wondered why,
he'd covered his tracks.

The only clue he failed
to erase was that one
bare fact. *Why*

*would you want to find
me?*

Why, I wondered,
don't you want
to be found?

୨

The world on the other side
was twice erased.

The first time, of course,
as smoke up the infamous
chimneys. The last,
sucked down the collapsed black hole
behind his eyes.

If you crossed its event horizon
you'd vanish too.

❦

I can understand his dead's resentments.

Left behind,
who wouldn't bear a grudge?

Sullen or not, though,
who else could I ask?

❦

— Why did the boychik's father cross the ocean?
— What was he running away from?
— Only us.

— Like you ran from taking over his store.

❦

Long before he boarded that boat
he'd crossed the ocean.

Long before it reached land
he'd disappeared.

ANEURYSM

All the family in my family
was on my mother's side.

I saw no evidence my father
ever had one. When I asked

where they were buried
my mother said, Where else?

Behind his eyes. They must have hated
it there, more crowded
than any cattle car or attic,
crammed into the frayed nerve fibers
of his brain. That vessel of blood
that finally burst was
how they escaped.

TRACES

Fifty-one million documents name the victims.
Seven hundred orphans dial their number every day.

And wait for someone to retrieve a scrap of paper.
And wait for a voice at the end of the line to tell them
how and when and where their relatives died.

Down to how many lice (they kept good records) crawled
on any given prisoner's head. Their number is etched
in my speed-dial, a shrine to the idol of closure.

I call it a dozen times a day. On hold I listen to a cantor chant
prayers for the dead. When I confess I can't spell their last names in
    Polish,
they assure me they've developed algorithms to correct for any gaps.

When I ask, "A gap so big it swallowed Poland? How many shovels
does it take to correct for that?" — they warn me not to get smart.
When I tell them the chain of custody was corrupted by my birth
they start to lose their patience, but add they might be able to help
if I gave them at least one name.
As if he ever spoke their names out loud.

Unless the furry syllables of his snores were some kind of code.
He napped every night after dinner, memories mulched
under the headlines folded over his face.

When they put me on hold again, a sales pitch loops
through the system — group excursions to Eastern Europe,
annotated tours of memory's ruins, very popular
with your second generation.

I correct the anonymous voice: I'm the last generation.
No digging through Polish potato fields for me.
I'm explaining myself long after the line's gone dead —

Lead an excursion to Poland-before-I-was-born
so I can bring them back alive, you can name your own price.

Take me back to when the rest of me still lived.
Before my father's amputations and my mother's missing milk.
Back before Hitler, that goes without saying.
Before Wagner and Bismarck and Luther. Germany, just to be sure.
Before the bloody battalions of holy hermits and saints.
The clean-up squads of Crusaders.
Before the expulsion from Spain.
Before Aquinas, Augustine and Paul, marching down the centuries
through our shtetls, shovels, mops and Bibles shoulder-high.
Before the Gospels.

Before God's wanton promise:
Seed as numberless as the flakes of ash crowning Poland's sky.

RIDDLE AND DITCH

MY FATHER'S EYES IN POLAND: RIDDLE AND DITCH

When my distance
from the disaster
dug the ditch that
drained
our lives

and dropped you

between walls as steep
as chimneys
no handholds
cracks or crannies

did you ever see
the sun or learn
to miss it?

૭

In my eyes

you were too late
to save them

unworthy
to replace them

with no business
being born
How much of you wasn't?

૭

Too poor to pay
their passage

Too distant to die
beside them

What gave me
the right
to survive?

❧

When the snow that fell
from my eyes
in Poland-before-
you-were-born
buried us both
alive under my dead
do you remember
which one of us first
turned blue and crazed?

❧

Where did the most
of you that wasn't
born wait his turn?

Against a stump
in Poland's forests?
On the ice
of Poland's swamps?

In Poland's fog?

૭

The ditch that divides
the living from the dead —

Could you ever tell
on which side
I'd left you
stranded?

૭

When I stacked my dead
in your crib like frozen logs
how long did it take
for the weight
to crush your eggshell chest?

૭

Did the scratching
of their fingernails
on its walls keep
you awake?

Could you read their names
through the bruises
where I scrubbed
the filth away?

૭

How could you sleep?

When my dead grew

like stalactites in the cave
of Poland's winter
and the shame
of my survival like
stalagmites in the cave
of Poland's night?

༄

When my eyes
snowed in Poland
and I tethered cold
blue horses to your crib

and threw scratchy blankets
over their flanks

did you feed them the hay
I stole from Poland's marshes?

༄

If I thaw the tongues
of my dead
will they absolve me?

༄

When my horses pulled
your crib like a sleigh
its runners scarring
the snow with a trail
of rust

and one horse
limped and its twisted
hoof splayed its broken
rhythm against
the ice

did you fear
you might spill out
or was that what you prayed for?

༄

When you cried
from thirst
and I gave you
a stone to suck
did you know each stone
was a name I couldn't
swallow? Each name
a stone stuck
halfway down my throat?

༄

When I crushed each name
to fine powder
stone on stone
and mixed it with Poland's ashes
and Poland's snow
and smeared the greasy paste
on your parched tongue
how did you swallow?
Did you keep the dead down
or vomit them up?

❧

The last two Jews
in Poland hid
in the snow
behind my eyes —

Did you learn
their language?

How to pin down
vowels that drift
between snow and sorrow?
Consonants crushed
under boot heels
and the iron wheels
of trains?

❧

How will you solve
my insoluble riddles?

I set a trapline
in the snow —

their steel jaws snap
shut as soon as you open
your mouth.

ALTERATIONS

MY GRANDMOTHER'S SEWING MACHINE

Don't think my mother doesn't know, as she bends her head
to the evening's alterations
on her stool at the back of her husband's tiny store,

that this sewing machine she will spend the night hunched over
is more precious than rubies.

She's read my grandmother's postcards —

As long as soldiers need uniforms
won't the Germans need women who sew?

Won't a woman with her own machine,
kept oiled and in good repair,
stay busy until Hitler's defeat?

She can't send her own machine to Poland.
Who knows if it would get there? Who can afford the freight?
And it's for her own alterations the customers flock to the store.

But how many months has it been
since the postcards stopped?
How many months
and they haven't come up with the cash
for a half-decent third-hand machine,
its best days long behind it?

They don't know what to think.

I could have told them.
Not that they asked.
Why would they?

It was months before I'd be born.

But I knew. I was a bundle
of eavesdropping nerves,
stewing in all the bad news
they kept from themselves.
I knew how these things turned out.
They always do.

All I could do was wave
a blind goodbye.

ANNE IN THE ATTIC

In the camps the Muselmanner
gave up first. You couldn't say
they were living, you couldn't say
they were dead. They were like
the mannequins who modeled clothes
in my father's store. One lived
in our attic. We called her Anne.
She even looked a little Dutch
with her blond wig and wooden
clogs. Not that she ever wore them.
She couldn't risk the noise.
The real Anne could have used
a wig like hers. She's been there ever since
I turned thirteen, the day my father
brought her home from his store. "It's time,"
he said, "you learned to live like a Jew.
Forget the rabbi's *narishkeit*.
She'll teach you everything you need
to know." Up the stairs to the tiny
attic; he locked us in.
In the camps all the Muselmanner
cared about was food. If you grabbed one
by the throat, it might collapse. They lived,
if you call that living, from finger to mouth.
They ran out of time before they could learn
the rules. Before he turned the key he gave
me a sandwich. "From your mother," he sighed,
as if I couldn't guess. "She worries you might get
hungry. Better she worries you won't learn
how to starve."

MY GRANDMOTHER'S HAIR

If you travel to Germany
tell me if you slept on my grandmother's hair.
You'd know — in the night
you would have heard the mattress rustle,

and the sigh, buried deep
in its stuffing:

my grandmother,
dreaming of me.

KAPUT

Had my father been forewarned,
had he had foreknowledge,
had a courier from Poland — or
an angel or a dove — whispered
in his ear, "No one in your family
will make it," he would have pulled out
in time and prevented me.

The *Hitlerschnitt* they call it,
in that land where the end
of his line began in line-ups
that stretch for blocks.
In the office where Jews
lean on counters to fill out
spurious forms.
Press down hard
on their pens to leave
an impression of a person
granted the right to exist.
While the desk clerk flicks
a switch and the secret machine
ticking quietly under the counter
shoots a steady stream of X-rays through
ovaries or testicles. In less time
than it takes to complete the form
the promised generations are erased.

His closest call
with the *schnitt*
was a nick at the root
of his tongue.
It wouldn't stop
bleeding. There went
all his words.

୬

By the time I was twelve he'd filled
my room with more shoes
than a child could wear.

The clerks slid my feet
into the bottom tray
of their polished wooden
cabinets to ensure a perfect
fit. The fluoroscopic X-rays lit
a fuse of slow decay.

It crept to my groin
from the green bones
of my feet. I loved
watching them glow
on the screen.

୬

The lab tech handed me the narrow glass vial
 and pulled out the yellow cork stopper
and gave me a few magazines to lend a helping hand
to my helping hand and pointed me down a long narrow
     hallway
that had just been repainted,

the pale green paint still a little sticky to the touch,
and pointed me to the privacy of a stall behind a door
that wouldn't lock.

When he slid my slide under the lens and it clicked into focus
I overheard him mutter he'd never seen so many flailing

broken necks

MANNEQUINS' GRAVEYARD

1.
My father's dress store depended
on women to keep us alive —
the customers and salesgirls, the mannequins

who modelled last year's styles.
I worked behind the counter after school,
punched the pleated cardboard boxes

into shape, lined them with crumpled tissue
to protect the precious dresses I delivered
on my bike. My mother did alterations.

When her sight went bad she entrusted me
to the salesgirls' nimble fingers. They knew
how to follow a pattern, how much

to let out or take in, their stitches invisible
and sure. At the back of the store,
at a long wooden workbench, where customers

weren't allowed, the girls with their scissors
and thimbles, needles and thread, pedalling
faster and faster, plotted the perfect fit.

The salesgirls had no husbands or sons. Once a year,
at the Christmas party table, they drank hard liquor
and plotted revenge. They propped me against

their pillows and dressed me like their doll.
The next day was their saviour's birthday; everything
was allowed.

2.
Was that where my father buried his brothers —
under the basement of his store? The scrape
of his shovel and pick rasped through my dreams.

Under the mannequins' graveyard — that pile
of tangled wigs, chipped smiles and broken limbs —
in the basement of the store his brothers stirred.

Impatient as ever, he'd yanked up the ladder
and left. My legs dangling over the edge
of their pit, a fishing-rod broom cradled in my hands,

my uncles taught me to fish and smoke
and dress like a man. Starting with mudcaked boots
for my feet, they worked their way up to my head.

THE PERFECT STONE

Six years after the war my father
waits on the beach for his dead.

In my parents' first store,
little more than a hallway,
the closet at the back held the sewing
machine on its spindly iron legs
where my mother did alterations,
letting down hems, taking in seams,
measuring, cutting, basting —
their customers, at war
with their bodies, relied
on my mother's needle to give them
a touch of glamour while I played
with the censored scraps that fell
at her feet. I raked them
into mountains, and when I got bored
I shovelled them into her lap
and when I got whiny she sewed
my map of the world.

Do you remember,
she asked me — my first geography
lesson — her thimbled finger trembling,
do you remember what this means?
I remembered. Red was danger,
like your palm pressed flat
on the stove or crossing the street.
And blue is where you drown.
I had to land on green, only green was safe.
Green — a few tiny freckles
scattered over the bubbling face
of the world. Green — barely big enough
for a fort to hide my toys in,

my cowboys and my Indians,
my soldiers and their guns.
Green — the little patch of sand
where I stood watch with my father.
They'd drowned in a boiling blue blob
she called Poland; we waited
on the shore of Lake St. Clair.
They'd burned in a big red fire
he called Europe. We waited
until the store closed,
our shadows long in the flames
of the setting sun.

My father taught me the secret
of skipping stones. First, he told me,
find the perfect stone: flat and thin,
not so light it won't skip; not so heavy
it sinks. It sits snug
between your thumb and index finger
stretched as far apart as they can stretch.
If you find the perfect stone, it will skip itself.

The perfect stone is green.
The lake is blue. The sky
is red. We wait for the lake to part,
we wait for the dolphins. We wait for his brothers
to break the waves, bareback on their soaring
stallions, yelling, laughing, exultant,
their six-guns blazing back at the wounded sun.
We wait.

I made
    thirteen   perfect
        skips
            in a row
                my lucky night.

Murray Reiss

UNANSWERED LETTERS

In the cradle of my skull I hear
dead tongues. My father's barbed
wire Yiddish, his letters home

to Poland, crowd the night. My mother
takes in alterations. Her feet work
the clattering pedals. She stitches

one word to the next. I listen
for the rustle of uncles and cousins
in her thread. A needle through

my tongue would make more sense.
She steams his letters flat
with her heavy iron. It hisses

in the night like the whispered
orders of men gathering at the door.
No one breaks down our door. No one

answers my father's letters.

BURIED IN A BOOK

I read the cereal box
at breakfast in English
and French. My father
piles lox on a bagel, gulps
his coffee, black, then drives
downtown in his midnight-blue DeSoto.

He opens his store
and I open another book.

He sells a dress, I turn
a few more pages.

He buries himself in his business,
I bury myself in a book.

I'm learning how to escape
between two covers.

He's showing me
you can do it in plain sight.

In front of a rack
of dresses instead of behind
a wall of words.

When I've turned
the last page
I have to come up for air.

When he opens the doors
on the day after Christmas
and the mob lined up

for the sale of the year
almost tramples him
in their rush, his punch-
drunk smile never wavers.

The one thing
we both agree on
is this beats being
buried alive.

Being lined up at the lip of a pit,
shoved over the edge by the butt
of a gun.

When playing dead's
your only chance
to cling to life.

WHITTLED AND FED

My mother wanted boatloads of children.
My father wanted to curl up and die.

Who knew from therapy? It was 1945.
And even if they did, who had the money?

You worked things out the best you could.
You gave a little here, took a little there …

She agreed to stop at me, he agreed to live.
This worked until it didn't.

She wanted more, he wanted less
and I kept getting bigger. Every plate

she placed in front of me made it worse.
My mother believed in addition — if one

was all she got, she'd cook for ten —
my father in subtraction: the less you were

the easier to hide. One built me up;
one whittled away.

BIG TOMATOES

My father refuses food from anyone's garden.
He knows how they grow those big tomatoes.
You dig a dead Jew in your soil.

That's how they did it in Poland
the year the postcards stopped.
That year of the bumper crops.
That year they fertilized their fields
with bone and ash.

Better the cans of soup that line the cellar.

Sometimes my mother can't help it.
She stomps a few seeds under her heel
and prays for rain.

If he catches her he calls her a *kapo*.
If she stoops to pull a weed
he pulls his hair. He remembers what happened
the last time they weeded Europe.

The disciplined ranks of tomatoes.
The cabbages in their rigid, orderly rows.
The peasants with their sharpened hoes and sickles.

Smoke from the trampled heaps of weeds in the ditches
still stings his eyes.

He refuses to let one tear
water the ground.

THE SURVIVAL RATE OF BUTTERFLIES IN THE WILD

THE SURVIVAL RATE
OF BUTTERFLIES IN THE WILD

There are no butterflies here in the ghetto.
— Pavel Friedmann, Theresienstadt, 4 June 1942

My father set me an insoluble riddle before I was born.

"Are butterflies Jewish?" wasn't it.

That would have been too easy.

A Pole a Jew and a butterfly sidle into a bar — a ramshackle building
with an exit in the ghetto and its entrance in the Aryan side of town,

an administrative screw-up whose solution is slowly working its way up
the occupation's baroque chains of command. You could cover its grimy walls

with all the memos. It's the smugglers' bar, the counterfeiters' bar,
the bar where all the hustlers run their scams. The bartender eyes

this unlikely trio and sighs, as if he's heard this joke before, "Boys … Whaddya want?"
The Jew's looking for someone to help him disappear, the Pole wants to score

a case of that black market Russki vodka, but he dabbles in
this and that
and he says, I know a guy who could help, you got zlotys, or
better, diamonds,

or even better, gold? The butterfly says: Watch this — and
disappears.
The Jew, the Pole and the bartender can't believe it — the
butterfly's disappeared

in front of their eyes. They turn the bar upside down but still
can't find him.
The bartender shakes his head and stands the Jew and the
Pole to a fresh round of drinks.

It was the next-to-last day my wife Karen and I had in Costa Rica. I'd picked up a flyer that morning for a butterfly farm not far outside of town. Knowing I had to see it, though I didn't yet know why, I cashed our next-to-last travellers' cheques and paid the forty dollars (US) for the tour. Who had time to shlep on local buses?

The little white van with the cheerfully smiling flower face decals stuck on its doors picked us up at the curb in front of the Grand Hotel and drove us to the butterfly farm at La Guácima.

Before the tour began they sat us down to watch a video in which animation and simultaneous translation let the butterflies themselves explain every turn of their complicated cycles of disclosure and disguise from larva to pupa to adult in Spanish, English, German, Italian and French:

"In the wild, friends, do you know how many — or should I say how few of us — survive to mate and reproduce? Less than two percent! And the rest? All the rest of us — yes, all but two percent — get eaten, or mauled, or die exhausted from the constant effort of maintaining our protective disguises."

In the October 1934 issue of the *Volksgesundheitswacht* ("The People's Health Guardian"), a Dr. Stahle announced new research concerning blood and race, citing a Russian scientist's claims to distinguish Jewish from Russian blood by chemical means with an accuracy of ninety-two percent. "Think what this means! We could identify non-Aryans in the test-tube! Neither deception, nor baptism, nor name change, nor citizenship, no not even nasal surgery could help them . . . One cannot change one's blood!"

At every stage of our life predators stalk us.

Beetles and birds devour our eggs whether we hide them on the underside of leaves or in the tiny cracks and chinks carved into bark.

Flies and wasps infest our larvae, burrow from within to destroy those the birds and beetles overlook.

Songbirds rear their nestlings on our larvae. The beauty of their melodies are fueled by our young.

This wasn't his riddle either:

A man has two Jewish grandparents, one Aryan grandmother and a half-Aryan grandfather; the latter was born Jewish and became Christian only later. Is this sixty-two percent Jewish person a Mischling (mixed breed) or a Jew?

Had it been, the answer would go like this:

According to the Nuremberg Laws the man is a Jew because of the one grandparent who was of the Jewish religion; this grandparent is assumed to have been a full Jew and this assumption cannot be contested. A sixty-two percent Jew has three full Jewish grandparents. If, on the other hand, the half-Aryan grandfather had been Christian by birth, he would not have been a full Jew and would not count for this calculation; his grandson would have been a Mischling of the First Degree.

Hornets and wasps, spiders and bugs suck our babies dry, chop them up into bite-sized bits they carry home to their nests.

Lizards and hornets, assassin and ambush bugs, dragonflies and spiders, ants and praying mantises all lie in wait for those few that emerge from their pupa.

And for those, even fewer, that grow into adults, crab spiders and tiger beetles lurk behind shrubs and bushes, frogs and toads and mice hunt us down.

In 1942, the American playwright and screenwriter Ben Hecht tried, and failed, to involve a group of Hollywood moguls in a campaign to have Congress establish an agency for the rescue of Europe's Jews. Each and every person Hecht approached told him that a Jew must be very careful not to antagonize the American people. A Jew, they insisted, at a time like this, must remain as invisible as possible.

✡

If I were a butterfly I'd be a pupa, no longer larval but not yet fully born.

Unable to bite or sting, fly or wriggle away.

I'd imitate bits of curled-up leaf, broken twigs or bark.

Mimic the end of a chewed-up leaf or bird shit.

Every pupa has its specialty.

If I were one I'd excel at playing dead.

✡

Here at the butterfly farm, though, workers with the gentlest hands protect us in cages of fine black mesh they set on the forest floor, in the dappled sun. When they return to harvest our eggs we gladly share them.

They stick our eggs to the leaves of host plants, tend each plant in a separate pot, set each pot in a separate cage, protecting first our eggs and then the hatched-out larvae from the wasps and ants and spiders and birds such a dense population inevitably attracts. No matter how fine or firmly anchored the mesh, they always find a way to creep in. Only the workers and the cages keep us safe.

Once our larvae can fly they release us into the display space, again enclosed in mesh, where you will stroll after we finish explaining these facts of life, a smear of ripe banana on your wrists to bring us close.

"Here at La Guácima," boasts the proud butterfly farm owner, elbowing a couple of giant morphos aside, "by taking all these measures, we have improved the odds of a butterfly surviving to mate and reproduce from two to ninety-three percent."

The survival rate of children in Poland whose clothing bore the mark of the yellow star varied — depending on your sources and who, for the purposes of this calculation, they counted as a child — but not by much. Most accounts agree: there had been just under a million children in 1939 and after the war no more than 5,000. Their rate of survival: one-half of one percent.

No one on our tour compares the butterfly farm to a ghetto. Why would they? Its purposes seem entirely benign. On the wildly popular excursions to the Third Reich's ghettos, German tourists were entertained by Jews forced to explain why in this, their natural state, they preferred not to bathe or feed their young. How, left to their own devices, they were so much happier wallowing in their filth. Tours on which, for a few extra pfennigs, the tourists were offered rare aesthetic experiences to photograph: "Public hangings. Fresh corpses, twisting in the wind. Capture the striking contrast between blue faces and black tongues."

✡

Should their surroundings grow so hostile that they offer no chance to hide or escape, a butterfly will retreat into diapause, a state of suspended animation, and wait it out until conditions change. If they ever do.

✡

Every pupa has its specialty.

Mine was blending in with my father's dead.

Extinct, my father's family crowded around my crib, their faces fog, their bodies smoke, their voices soft and insistent as the flutter of butterfly wings.

They'd gathered to offer their last descendant
a few survival tips

because when the *lantslaite* knocked at my father's door and tried to tell him,

when they shuffled their feet and pulled at their long grey beards and tried to tell him,

when they coughed in their gabardine sleeves, adjusted their fur-trimmed hats, pulled at their unruly *payess* and finally told him
that of his family no one else still lived
that he alone was left

repeated that of his family no one survived the camps

he stared at my mother's bulging belly

and asked me, Then why should you?

And once I had

and he rocked and swayed, squeezed his head in his hands, and lamented, "It should have been me instead," they warned me not to remind him I was alive.

It reminds him we are not. You don't want that.

Disguise yourself as one of us — that was their best advice.

Whose own disguises failed in the end.

Who had stumbled over their prayers.
Fumbled the sign of the cross.
Mangled the way the locals spoke their Polish.

Their disguises no match for the prying eyes of suspicious
    neighbours,
for the Jew-sniffing noses of death-squad dogs,
in the end their rate of survival flatlined at zero.

They tried to reassure me:
We've learned from our mistakes.

Make your face like fog and your body smoke
and your voice a distant whisper from the bottom
of Poland's swamps and your father will pass you over.
You just might get away with being alive.
When I asked them how long I would have to play dead,
they admitted they didn't know.

The video over, I stroll out into the enclosure, a smear of ripe banana on my wrist for the morphos and glasswings, the longwing tigers, monarchs and owls, who envelop me in an iridescent cloud of shimmering wings.

A fluttering cloud, from which familiar voices call.
A little raspy, a little wispy,
I haven't heard them since they surrounded my crib.

Yoo hoo boychick — surprised to see us here?
Surprised? I'm astounded.
Well don't be.
By the way, you're looking good
Why so surprised?
He's never read the Cabala?
Doesn't know about the transmigration of souls?
Never read Isaac the Blind? Or the Baal Shem Tov?

> I've read the Baal Shem Tov, a few of the stories.
> When I was a Buddhist for a while, I believed in reincarnation.
> But butterflies?
> What are you doing here?

We drifted across the ocean.
Smoke travels.
We found this place.
We liked it.
So we stayed.

You saw the show. See how good they protect us.
It's warm, it's safe. We eat, we sleep,
there's flowers.
Everybody comes here, they got nothing better to do,
all day they wander around

their forearms smeared with ripe banana.
What's better than that?

    What can I say? It beats Miami Beach.

But enough about us, boychick, look at you.
Did you ever stop playing dead?

The Jew and the Pole are on their fourth round of vodka,
still trying to figure it out, when the butterfly suddenly pops
    back up.

Where the fuck were you? they ask. Right here
all the time, he casually answers.

Those cigarette stubs . . . ? That ash spilling out of the
    ashtray . . . . ?
Those wet rings of vodka smeared all over the table …?

You call that a joke?
my father asks.

That wasn't his riddle either.

SECOND-HAND SURVIVOR

SECOND-HAND SURVIVOR

My father fell victim to second-hand smoke
decades before his condition had a name.

His distance from the chimneys didn't spare him;
his distance from those smokestacks was his disease.

EMPTY FRAMES

The decisive event of my father's life
was his absence from it.

He was here instead of there
and then I was too.

Two of us was one too many.
My mother could nurse only one thirst at a time.

I pour her missing milk into his empties,
drink myself to sleep and board the train

that whisks me away to Poland-before-I-was-born.

At the platform, I wait under cold glass stars
and a jagged moon. The platform

shakes when they pry the sealed doors open.
He shakes me awake every morning, search-

lights in my eyes, hunting for
the passengers he expects to welcome home.

As she dresses me for school, my mother complains:
"You want him to find them, show him their pictures."

"Pictures? Let him look in the mirror."
"It isn't fair." He hates it when I whine.

"None of them look like me —
their faces are broken."

"You'll look like them," he promises,
"just wait."

PRAYER

We have a prayer where I come from
for when death stormed through with his Zyklon-B
and his scythe

For when you dust yourself off
survey the scene and conclude
a mistake has been made

It rumbles like a dormant volcano
at the bottom of our throats
We tamp it down like nitroglycerine
in the mezuzah on our doorjamb
Gouge it into our tefillin
until the leather groans and bleeds
And we wind them around our foreheads
tight as migraines

Bow and sway and mumble
beat our breasts and tear our hair
turn our backs on the living
throw in our lot with the dead
wail and plead
complain and insist —

It should have been me,
me instead.

WHO COULD ARGUE?

"Life goes on."

What could be more self-evident?
Who could argue with that?

My father.

And if you told him:
"Of course it goes on,
what else can it do?"
He'd answer: "It shouldn't."
It should have had the sense
to stop the moment
it stopped
making sense.
The second it floated
up the chimneys.
The instant their ash
struck the ground.

And if the trees refuse
to uproot themselves
and the seas to boil
themselves dry —

the decency to stop
before my birth.

A miscarriage
he could have coped with,
a stillbirth he would have taken
in his stride.

But a face that looked
like theirs
that wasn't them
he could only face

with a face stunned
into stone.

Life *hadn't* stopped in its tracks
and repealed itself?
It *hadn't* had the sense
to undo my birth?

FACES LIKE MINE

There *are* men in this
world whose faces look

like mine. I have seen them but
only through smoke.

We share my father's
hunted stare, stand speechless

in the temple
of the tongue and run

like water
from the crush of marching

boots.
I find them in the forest

and lose them
when the first bird calls.

Their faces turn
like mine to the waning sun,

on our eyelids fall
the ash of torn pages.

EARLIEST RIVALS

I used to think my earliest
rival was my parents' best friends'
son, but now I suspect

his parents. It was after the war
and my father was busy shopping
for replacements. For reasons

never explained to me, I didn't fit
the bill. They'd survived the camps.
Who could compete with that?

Not my father. Who knew what
to call his stunned condition? Any pain
he could claim paled next to theirs.

Three mannequins preened in his storefront
window. More than he could afford
for a struggling store. He'd printed numbers

on their wrists in indelible ink. On his own
the scars were barely healed.
When he took my hand I could feel

their fevered ridge. The mannequins' hands
were cool and smooth — Muselmanner,
they'd given up on life. My rivals

wore their shirt sleeves long, their voices
buttoned, buried their memories in a place
they'd never find. My father had none

of his own so he couldn't sleep. He prowled the small-town
streets until first light, asking the stop signs how and where
and when his brothers died. He needed to rub himself raw

against the crime. They'd been there; they could tell him
what it was like. They tried; the problem was:
they had survived. They could tell him what it was like —

up to a point. The point where the kapos shoved
the naked bodies through the doors
and an unseen hand poured in the Zyklon-B.

The point where his naked brothers
always disappeared from my father's sight.

I had no need to worry about my rivals.
They were as useless, in the end, as his only son.

BLUNT SHOVEL

For my thirteenth birthday
my father gave me a shovel.
"If you want to dig up Poland,
be my guest." I took him at his word —
my mistake. In our yard the dirt
was barely inches deep. Under that, a continent
of rock. When I turned fourteen
my present was a file.

THE LAST TWO JEWS IN POLAND

My father holds them for questioning
in the cage behind his eyes.

He's exhausted his list of suspects.
He's down to material witnesses, last seen
at the scene of the crime,
grilling them for particulars,
avid for details, facts.

"Tell me where they died,
was it Auschwitz or Belsen?
Tell me how they died,
were they shot or gassed?
Tell me where they hid,
in a closet or forest?
Tell me who betrayed them,
a Pole or a Jew?
You were there.
Don't spare me nothing.
I have ways
of making you talk."

Except he doesn't.

They've traded in their tongues for hands
and shoulders, speak only through elaborate
helpless shrugs.

They don't resemble any Jews he knows.
When he asks how they survived
(of course he's suspicious)
they pull a thick white blanket
over their heads.

He tugs a corner
and its edges unravel
in rags of snow.

Because the last two Jews in Poland cannot answer my
 father's grief
they drag their shivering fingers
through the snow.

One draws stick figures climbing up and down chimneys
and the other smoothes them away.

Because the last two Jews cannot answer his grief
he hands them shovels.
"Dig," he tells them," "in the snow
behind my eyes. Find a bone
from a wrist or a finger.
Tell me which way it points.
A handful of chattering teeth
will win your freedom."

When their shovels strike a rock he hears
skulls speak.

STATION, SCARECROW, TWIN

IN POLAND BEFORE I WAS BORN: CLUBFOOT TWIN

Soon after I become a man
in the eyes of the absconded God and my gassed forefathers
my father takes my hand and tells me the truth:

"You have a clubfoot twin I left behind in Poland
where he limps through fields and forests
searching for graves."

Is he that half of my life that was over
before it began?

All summer my mother labours in her garden. She divides
    her roots
and harvests her bitter herbs.

She insists, "You are and have always been
my only son."

Come winter my father tosses me a puck: "I spent your
    childhood
squeezing this from the coal of Poland's night."

He kneels to tie the laces of my skates in the double knot.
My mother rearranges her rows of preserves.

My twin and I add up to a double *no*:
one of us can't quite live and one can't die.

His straight foot points to the end of our fathers' line,
his twisted foot points backwards to the ramp

where we were one and with a flick of a finger
he was sent to the left and I to the right.

In his name my father reminds me, "You are only half a son,"
and tosses the coal-black puck down the frozen river.

The map he is always revising shows
how it drains our backyard rink into Poland's swamps.

He wants us whole
as if it doesn't matter

which half of us will live
and which half die.

MENGELE HAD TO LOVE

Mengele had to love us, me
and my clubfoot twin.

One of us born in Poland, the other across the sea,
yet here we are on his ramp at the same time.

"How can this be?" What experiments he devised
just for us. "You my little ones, you are among my chosen.

My little dead ringers, you will be spared the gas.
Yidkins, for you I will build the first cyclotron. How fast

to accelerate the particle beams before they rip you apart?
But for now, my little dizygotic lambkins, let's see you run.

Faster. Faster! Do I have to whip you? Run!
Yes, look — one limps and one stays steady, yes,

and look — they are joined at the foot. By a thin
hinge of cartilage and bone. What is this mysterious link?

How does it both join and separate?"
I could have told him if he'd asked

but that wasn't his way. "Let us see, if I hold
this membrane here and twist it there, hold and twist

once more, and yes! — it snaps. And one of them flops
like a fish and the other stops breathing. Such amusing
    antics.

When I write this up I shall call it, "The Fish-Boy and the
    Cyanotic Yid."

Murray Reiss

Even Mengele missed our secret. I live his clubfoot death

for him in Poland. When I skate down Sarnia's ponds
he limps at my side.

UNDER THE WIRE

Always the most incurable children
my mother fell in love with. She haunted hospital hallways

for the three years before I was born
demanding she be allowed to take one home.

As if to prove she could rescue someone
from the certified jaws of death,

as if to prove this wasn't Sarnia, wasn't 1942, then '43, then '44,
that the barbed wire wasn't strangling Poland,

the red tape sealing the mouths of Canada's harbours
hadn't wrapped itself around her thwarted womb.

Tanks rolled across the headlines; on the back page,
under rows of tiny Anglo-Saxon print, they buried Jews.

She knew what it meant when the postcards stopped.
With wool and cotton rationed, facts in short supply,

an inventory their little dress store was running out of,
she argued blood and money with her husband every night,

crossed out the names they'd scribbled on scraps of paper,
argued who should live and who would die.

Every night he did the books; they never balanced.
On his side brothers pleading to be rescued;

on her side strangers pressing to be born. One more night
with rescue, if rescue still there was, beyond his means.

They slept, if sleep there was, in severed dreams.
His brothers slip through the petrified trees of Poland's
    forests,

black hair bleached a streaky, dirty blonde,
past dozing guards and drowsy dogs, fake passports bulging

with forged visas pressed to their hearts.
She pushes through the emergency exit of a hospital hallway,

oblivious to the alarm bells, ignoring shouts of "Stop!"
her stolen treasure harboured in her arms.   I was the one

they saved but they never noticed the mud
still caked on my ankles, the scars — still red, still weeping —

where the barbed wire raked my back.

BOARDING TIME

My father drops me off at the station.
He's sharpened my skates to bite

the necklace of frozen swamps.
He can't resist reminding me one last

time: "Don't get off until the train's pulled
into Poland." He pins a note for the conductor

to my sleeve. It doesn't matter. This train
only travels to Poland-before-I-was-born.

It speeds down the ditch the dead
dig behind his eyes. It glides through time's

scarred tunnel as if on skates. This train can't stop
till it reaches the end of the line.

When it crosses the border I unfold my map,
 watch its landmarks resurrect outside the window.

A hushed valley filled with fog
drifted in from the marshes.

A hundred blue horses lined up
inside a fence.

Mounds of black beards and sidelocks,
raided by birds for their nests.

Clay ovens where loaves of braided bread
await the Sabbath queen.

A well and a pail and a garden.
A frozen pond.

HOW TO PLAY HUNT AND HIDE

Watch out for when it begins.
It begins before you know it.
You need a head start.

There are three teams
playing against you.
Each team has its rules.

The Hunters are one team.
They never let up.
When they find you
they can kill you.
That's their rule.

The second team
is every Hider
who's bigger than you.
If they fear you'll give them away
they can kill you too.

The third team is your body.
It could betray you at any time.
You never know.

You have one simple rule.
Learn it by heart:
You can't let anyone know
you are alive.

You can act like you're already
dead, or pretend
you've never been born.
It's up to you.

You might win if you teach
your body to do without food.
It won't whimper with hunger
if it doesn't need to eat.

You might win if you teach
your body to do without
water. Its throat
won't rattle with thirst
if you don't need to drink.

Better still, do without
breathing. Make your body
that quiet and you're much
more likely to win.

You can't come out
until the game is over.
Wait for a whistle or siren.
Someone will announce
when it's the end.

Don't come out if they say
the Hunters won.

You have to know
who to believe
before you come out.

You get double points
for finding
your former body.

Triple if you can bring it
back to life.

STATION, SCARECROW, TWIN

1

I find myself at the end of the line
waiting to board a train with my clubfoot twin.
The engines are snowing and the moonlight is broken
in two by their hesitant hum. The station looks almost
    abandoned,
weeds climb up the wall. It's the first time we've met
and he hands me his suitcase, a blood-red leather valise,
and a portrait in a pewter frame: two children —
the daughter who drowned and the son the fire claimed;
both of us at the end of our father's line. We ask for two
    tickets
to Poland on the train that goes back in time.
The conductor says come back tomorrow; can't we see
night closing in? Behind us the tracks
shine with a second skin of bone-white ice.
In a perfect world
he would never have left my side.

2

He buries our father's pitchfork
in a mound of smouldering hay, feed for the horses
who haul this winter's dead, our garden's perennial crop.
Mice nibble

the feet of the scarecrow
he stuffed with last year's straw.
Four crows, unruffled, peck
at its coal-black eyes, twin lumps
that mirror mine.

I remember the hospital hallways.
I remember asking the doctors
where he had gone. They said
his illness had no cure
this side of Poland;
they sent him there to be nursed
by my father's lost tribe.

He drags his foot and scribbles
riddles in the snow:

Two golden-haired boys. One pitchfork between them.
How many times do they stab the haystack
before they find
a Jew?

A different two boys. One bucket between them. Hair black
as coal. How much mud do they have to haul to bury
the dead floating belly-up
in their father's eyes?

POSTCARDS FROM POLAND: PRAYERS

My father pasted them on the walls
of our cramped apartment in neat

chronological rows: Invasion. Occupation.
Ghetto. Then the first hesitant rumours

of the camps — postcards from Poland,
every other word *rescue* or *help*. I lay in my crib

while he paced their circuit, condemning himself
in the voices of his dead. All he had left of them:

lines of faded ink. Not even enough to knot
into a noose. At night the postcards whispered

to themselves. Words were not what I heard
but the rustle of bodies, rising from crushed

consonants and vowels. They were nine.
I made a *minyan*. They were willing to overlook

my tender age. Now they could pray
for my father to let them go. They didn't know that the air

in my father's house was clotted with unanswered prayers.
How could their pleas rise to the ceiling,

let alone soar through the roof? In my father's house,
were prayers answered, they would be alive instead of him.

FATHER YOUR VILLAGE

   1

My father is a stone in a field of women.
It rains all day but they do not share their water.

My father is a stone in a field of women.
The moon is full but they make his bed in shadow.

My father is a stone in a field of women.
The wind moans but they won't repeat its stories.

   2

Father your village in Poland gone
who will mourn with you now
Family neighbours enemies gone
who will mourn with you now
Cheders shops and synagogues gone
who will mourn with you now
Every last Jew in Poland gone
who will mourn with you
who is your village now

> A field of stones
> Rub them together
> These stones will curdle milk

Who will teach them to sing
and give them tongues

> A field of stones is my village
> Stuff them in my pockets
> Let them drag me to the bottom
> of Poland's swamp

Who will paint these stones
with faces that look like yours

With eyes that look on the living
as well as the dead

> A field of stones is my village
> Heavier than extinction
> We pass them from hand to hand

Who will roll away the stone
that seals the tunnel
your dead dig home to Poland every night
Who will roll away the stone
at the mouth of your mouth

> My village is a field of stones
> at the end of the line
> Plant them
> The dead will root again in Poland's mud

Father your eyes that snow in Poland
cannot hold your dead
They spill out every night
They crowd my crib
Their voices coat my tongue
with flakes of ash
Take up your shovel
Dig them a place of rest

> Even their eyelids and fingernails gone
> How can I bury my dead
> Even their hair and ashes gone
> How can I bury my dead
> Every stone of my village gone
> How can I bury my dead

3
If they live in me

NOTES

"Traces"
The International Tracing Service in Bad Arolsen serves victims of Nazi persecutions and their families by documenting their fate through the archives it manages. The alphabetically and phonetically arranged Central Name Index contains over 50 million reference cards for over 17.5 million people.

"My Grandmother's Hair"
In the early 1940s there was a brisk trade between felt and textile manufacturers in Germany and the death camps in Eastern Europe.

"The Survival Rate of Butterflies in the Wild"
In the October 1934 issue . . . Saul Friedlander, *Nazi Germany and the Jews: The Years of Persecution*
A man has two Jewish grandparents. . . Friedlander
In 1942, when the American playwright . . . Aviva Cantor, *Jewish Women Jewish Men*
The Third Reich's ghettos . . . Friedlander, *Nazi Germany and the Jews: The Years of Extermination*

GLOSSARY

Cheder — religious school.

Goyim — Christians.

Hitlerschnitt — "Hitler's cut," slang for eugenic sterilization.

Kapos — concentration camp prisoners who were given power over other inmates to carry out Nazis' orders.

Lantslaite — people from the same home town in the old country.

Mezuzah — a tiny box affixed to the right side of the doorway of Jewish homes containing a portion of Deuteronomy, handwritten on parchment.

Minyan — the smallest number of adult Jews (which includes boys over thirteen) who constitute a congregation for communal religious services and prayers.

Muselmanner — death camp slang for prisoners on the edge of death who had surrendered to their fate.

Narishkeit — nonsense.

Payess — long side-curls worn by Hasidic and other ultra-Orthodox Jewish men.

Petseleh — little penis.

Tefilin — two small black boxes with black straps attached to them containing verses from the Torah; Jewish men are required to place one box on their head and tie the other one on their arm each weekday morning.

Murray Reiss was born in Sarnia, Ont., and lives on Salt Spring Island, BC, with his wife Karen, a ceramic sculptor. Since moving to Salt Spring in 1979 he's been a special education teacher and child care worker, and coordinator of the Salt Spring Water Council. He currently works as a freelance editor and environmental writer. His poetry and prose have been published in literary magazines and anthologies in Canada and the United States. His chapbook, *Distance from the Locus*, was published by Mothertongue Press in 2005. He also performs with singer-songwriter Phil Vernon as the "folkenword" duo Midnight Bridge.

Samuel Bak (cover artist) is a distinguished Jewish painter. Born in Vilna in 1933, his first exhibition was at the age of nine during the Nazi occupation of the Vilna Ghetto. At this time massive executions of Jews were taking place almost every day, but he and his mother managed to escape. He later worked as an artist in Israel, Paris, Rome, Switzerland, and the US. Many of his paintings arise from his experience of the Holocaust. Publications on his work include twelve books, most notably a 400-page monograph entitled *Between Worlds*, and his touching memoir, *Painted in Words*. He has also been the subject of several documentary films.